Harry & Meghan

Harry & Meghan

Making Their Own Way

2nd Edition

PERCY LEED

LERNER PUBLICATIONS ◆ MINNEAPOLIS

Lerner Publications Company
An imprint of Lerner Publishing Group, Inc.
241 First Avenue North
Minneapolis, MN 55401 USA

For reading levels and more information, look up this title at www.lernerbooks.com.

Main body text set in Rotis Serif Std 55 Regular. Typeface provided by Adobe Systems.

Editor: Annie Zheng **Designer:** Connie Kuhnz

Library of Congress Cataloging-in-Publication Data

Names: Leed, Percy, 1968– author.
Title: Harry and Meghan : making their own way / Percy Leed.
Description: 2nd edition. | Minneapolis : Lerner Publications, [2024] | Series: Gateway
    biographies | Includes bibliographical references and index. | Audience: Ages 9–14 |
    Audience: Grades 4–6 | Summary: "In 2016 Prince Harry and then American actress Meghan
    Markle began dating. Explore the couple's first meeting, their journey after marriage, and
    their adjustment to life after stepping away from the duties of the royal family"– Provided by
    publisher.
Identifiers: LCCN 2023022644 (print) | LCCN 2023022645 (ebook) | ISBN 9798765624036
    (library binding) | ISBN 9798765624081 (paperback) | ISBN 9798765624050 (epub)
Subjects: LCSH: Harry, Prince, Duke of Sussex, 1984—-Juvenile literature. | Meghan, Duchess
    of Sussex, 1981—-Juvenile literature. | Royal couples–Great Britain–Biography–Juvenile
    literature. | Monarchy–Great Britain–History–21st century–Juvenile literature. | Princes–
    Great Britain–Biography–Juvenile literature.
Classification: LCC DA591.A45 H46478 2024 (print) | LCC DA591.A45 (ebook) | DDC
    941.0860922–dc23

LC record available at https://lccn.loc.gov/2023022644
LC ebook record available at https://lccn.loc.gov/2023022645

Manufactured in the United States of America
1-1009632-51853-8/2/2023

Table of Contents

Harry and Meghan speak onstage during a humanitarian event in 2021.

On the night of the worldwide Netflix premiere of *Harry & Meghan* in December 2022, millions of viewers tuned in to watch the former royal couple's documentary series. The first episode set the tone for the series, beginning with the pair seated on a gray couch inside of a house in Santa Barbara, California.

Harry and Meghan are one of the world's most famous couples. In 2018 Harry, the grandson of Queen Elizabeth and sixth in line to the throne, walked the steps of St. George's Chapel in England with Meghan on their wedding day. Two years later, they left the royal family. Ever since their big exit in 2020, people have kept asking the same question: What happened?

The British royal family has always been fascinating to many people, and Harry and Meghan had a special appeal. They were a power couple made up of firsts: the first American to marry into the royal family since 1937, first woman of color in the modern British monarchy, and first couple to separate from the royal family. After their exit, media outlets speculated about what led to their fallout. Harry and Meghan had even given interviews to tell a small side of their story.

But this Netflix documentary series was different. Instead of allowing the press to spin their story, Harry and Meghan controlled the narrative. For the first time, they were able to openly tell their story the way they wanted it told. "No one knows the full truth. We know the full truth," said Harry. Around the globe, people followed the documentary series closely and watched as Harry and Meghan laid it all bare for the world to see.

Office workers watching Harry and Meghan's Netflix documentary

Princess Diana carrying
young Harry

Born a Royal

Prince Henry Charles Albert David was born on
September 15, 1984, in London, England. Everyone calls
him Harry. Harry is the second child of Charles and
Diana, then Prince and Princess of Wales. Harry's older
brother, William, was born in 1982. His grandmother was
Elizabeth II, then queen of the United Kingdom.

Growing up in the spotlight wasn't always easy. But
Harry's mother, Diana, did her best to make sure her
children had normal childhood experiences. She kept
William and Harry away from the press. She tried to show
them what life was like outside of royal palaces and estates.

The British Monarchy

The monarchy is the oldest form of government in the United Kingdom, which includes the countries of England, Scotland, Wales, and Northern Ireland. At one time, the king or queen ruled these nations by making laws. These days, the United Kingdom is a constitutional monarchy in which the king or queen is the chief representative of the country but cannot make laws. Parliament is the legislative branch that writes and passes laws.

They would take the bus in London; shop at Marks & Spencer, a British department store; and eat at McDonald's. But as members of the royal family, they also had a duty to visit foreign countries and attend official events.

In contrast to their royal lives, Diana exposed William and Harry to the difficulties that many people experienced. She showed them that it was important to help people who were less fortunate. Diana took her boys to hospitals and shelters for the unhoused. She was dedicated to helping others, and she wanted to make sure that her boys understood that they could help too.

When Harry was eleven, Charles and Diana announced their divorce. The two had been having problems in their marriage for some time, and the couple had separated a few years earlier. Their divorce became a scandal that was in the news daily, and Harry had difficulty escaping the gossip. Paparazzi aggressively followed and photographed the family wherever they went.

Left to right: Charles Spencer (Diana's brother), William, Harry, and Charles at Diana's funeral

In August 1997, Diana died in a car crash in Paris, France. The boys were vacationing with their father in Balmoral Castle in Scotland. When William and Harry, who were just fifteen and twelve years old, woke up later that morning, Charles delivered the terrible news.

Harry and William were devastated. Later that day, Charles took his sons to church so that they could reflect on their mother's death. The family stayed in Scotland to grieve privately as they made funeral arrangements.

Meanwhile, rumors spiraled about the cause of the crash. Paparazzi were following Diana's car, hoping to capture a picture of the former princess. Diana; her romantic partner, Dodi Fayed; and the driver died in the crash. After an investigation, the driver was blamed for the accident. However, the driver had been trying to lose the paparazzi following them. Harry, already annoyed by the photographers who followed him daily, became even more resentful of the constant cameras.

The United Kingdom was in mourning. People there and around the world loved Diana. They remembered her as incredibly warm, kind, and generous. Diana's funeral aired on televisions across the world. William and Harry, along with other relatives, walked behind her casket during the procession.

Charles kept William and Harry out of the public eye after the funeral. Though he has a hard time talking about his mother, Harry misses her and thinks of her daily. "Every day, depending on what I'm doing, I wonder what it would be like if she was here, and what she would

Asking for Help

Harry was just twelve years old when his mother died. As a member of the royal family, he tried not to show his emotions in public. To cope, Harry tried to shut down his emotions entirely. But years later, he realized that not talking about his mother's death was hurting him. So, in his late twenties, he sought out mental health therapy.

Therapy made a big difference in Harry's life. That's

say, and how she would be making everybody else laugh," he reflected. "Who knows what the situation would be, what the world would be like, if she were still around."

In 1998 Harry began attending secondary school (high school) at Eton College in Berkshire. While there, sixteen-year-old Harry got into trouble. He drank alcohol despite being under the legal drinking age, and he also tried marijuana, an illegal drug in the United Kingdom. His behavior made headlines, and reporters called him the Party Prince. After he admitted his offenses to his father, Charles made him visit a South London drug clinic. Harry got an up-close look at the dangers that come from substance abuse.

After that, Harry started acting more responsibly. He joined the Combined Cadet Force, a military-themed youth organization. While there, he found that the military life appealed to him. After secondary school, he applied and got

why Harry, along with his brother and sister-in-law, started Heads Together. This charity educates people about mental health issues and encourages people to seek help. It provides resources and assistance for people with mental health issues. Though Harry is no longer actively part of Heads Together, he still advocates for mental health and engages in projects that support it.

into the Royal Military Academy Sandhurst, the British Army's officer training center.

But before heading to Sandhurst, Harry took what's called a gap year. Many European students take a gap year, or a year to travel the world before continuing school or beginning a career. He spent part of his gap year in Africa. In Lesotho, Harry worked at an orphanage for children with AIDS, a disease caused by the HIV virus, which attacks the immune system. Harry's mother had devoted much of her time to bringing awareness to AIDS, so Harry wanted to continue her work.

Harry helping build a fence at an orphanage in Lesotho

Military Man

After returning to England from his gap year, Harry attended his father's wedding to Camilla Parker Bowles on April 9, 2005. The following month, Harry began his training at the Royal Military Academy Sandhurst.

He graduated from his special training course and joined a squadron that was due to deploy to Iraq in 2007. But after his deployment plans became public, British military leaders decided not to send Harry's unit. They thought Harry's presence would make the unit a target, endangering his life and the lives of other soldiers.

Harry was bitterly disappointed that he could not serve his country in Iraq. Later that year, British media outlets agreed not to publish details about Harry's next deployment. This would allow the prince's location to remain a secret from enemy forces. In December 2007, Harry began serving a tour of duty in Afghanistan.

But just two months after his deployment, news outlets broke the story that Harry was in Afghanistan, and he was recalled from duty. "I felt very resentful. . . . I felt as though I was really achieving something. I have a deep understanding of all sorts of people from different backgrounds and felt I was part of a team. I also wasn't a Prince, I was just Harry."

Harry visiting the British Royal Navy's fleet

Upon his return to England, Harry decided to train as an Apache helicopter pilot. The position would make it harder for the press to track him on the battlefield, while still allowing him to serve on the front lines. Harry trained with the Army Air Corps starting in 2009.

Harry took a brief break from training in 2011 for William's wedding to Catherine (Kate) Middleton. Harry attended the wedding with his then girlfriend, Chelsy Davy. He was delighted to welcome Kate into the family.

Harry (*back left*) leaves the chapel with the newly married couple (*front*), William and Kate.

Harry visits a school in Soweto, South Africa, as part of his royal tour in 2015.

After ten years serving in the British Army, Harry decided to end his military career in 2015. He loved the job, in part because it got him out of the limelight as a member of the royal family. But it also taught him to work hard and support his fellow soldiers. That sense of friendship and loyalty was invaluable to him.

He focused on charity work after leaving the military. Harry always felt a connection with the people in Africa, especially in Lesotho. Harry has often said he feels more himself in Africa than anywhere else. "I have this intense sense of complete relaxation and normality here. To not get recognized, to lose myself in the bush with . . . people [dedicated to conservation] with no ulterior motives, no agendas, who would sacrifice everything for the betterment of nature."

Free of his military duties, Harry had more time to spend with his family too. William and Kate had two young children, George and Charlotte. Harry adored his nephew and niece, and he was beginning to consider starting a family of his own one day. But first, he had to meet the right person.

Young Meghan

Rachel Meghan Markle was born in Los Angeles, California, on August 4, 1981. Her mother, Doria, is a social worker and yoga instructor. Her father, Tom, works in the television industry as a lighting and photography director. While her legal first name is Rachel, everyone calls her Meghan.

The family lived in Hollywood. Her father picked her up after school and often took her to the set of the sitcom he worked on, *Married with Children*. It was her introduction to the entertainment industry.

Meghan's racial identity has shaped her life in many ways. Meghan is biracial: her mother is Black, and her father is Caucasian. She didn't look much like her mother, so some people assumed Doria wasn't Meghan's mom. At that time, biracial families were less accepted by some

Meghan and her mother attend the 2017 Invictus Games in Toronto.

people. But Meghan's parents tried to make her feel that their family wasn't any different from other families.

When she was seven years old, Meghan asked for a set of Barbie dolls. She wanted a family set that included a mother, father, and two children. The dolls were sold as either all-white families or all-Black families. But when Meghan opened her gift on Christmas morning, she found a set with a Black mother and a white father. Her dad had bought both sets and created a family of dolls that looked like their family.

Meghan found a love for acting by starring in school plays at Immaculate Heart High School. She was in several productions at the all-girls school and in *Damn Yankees* at a neighboring school for boys. One of Meghan's former teachers, Christine Knudsen, remembers her as someone who loved to sing and dance and who had a lot of inner strength. Other teachers remember Meghan as a good student who had compassion for people in need, such as unhoused people and former gang members.

After high school, Meghan went to Northwestern University in Illinois. She loved acting, but she also loved politics. Meghan was conflicted about choosing a major. So she decided to combine her two passions and double-majored in theater and international relations.

Meghan is passionate about social issues around the world. In her junior year, she applied and was accepted for an internship at the US Embassy in Buenos Aires, Argentina. She worked for several months at the embassy. She immersed herself in her work and in the Spanish language so she could better communicate with Argentinians. It was a very exciting time, and Meghan was sure she would end up having a career in politics.

When she returned home, however, a friend put Meghan in touch with an entertainment manager. He saw a student film that Meghan had performed in and took her on as a client. In 2002 Meghan appeared in her first television role. She was in the background on the afternoon soap opera *General Hospital*. It wasn't much of a role, but she hoped it would lead to an acting career.

Making It in Hollywood

Meghan graduated from Northwestern University in 2003. After graduating, she returned home to Los Angeles and started looking for work as an actor. She had a few early successes: guest roles on television shows such as *Century City* and *CSI: NY*. But for the most part, she struggled to find acting roles. Part of her difficulty landing work came from her biracial identity. She looked ethnically ambiguous: not quite white and not quite Black. She went to auditions where they were casting for Latina, Black, or Caucasian roles. But despite continuing to get invitations to auditions, she failed to land the parts. "I wasn't Black enough for the Black roles and I wasn't white enough for the white ones, leaving me somewhere in the middle as the ethnic chameleon who couldn't book a job," she stated.

Meghan walks the red carpet for a *Suits* event.

That changed in 2011 when Meghan landed her first big role on the USA Network television show *Suits*. Producers were just looking to fill the role of a beautiful and confident woman who was an expert in law. They didn't specify a race. After her audition, the producers chose Meghan for the role. Meghan says the role is "the Goldilocks of my acting career—where finally I was just right." It was a long way from her days of working on a game show or as a background character on a soap opera.

Meghan's character on *Suits* was also biracial. At the end of the second season of the show, the producers cast her character's father as a Black man, played by Wendell Pierce. Many viewers did not realize that Meghan and the character she played were biracial, and the casting of her father surprised viewers. Some said offensive things about Meghan after they found out she was biracial. Their reactions brought public attention to the racism that many people of color face in the United States.

Meghan has used her platform as a television star to speak out on issues that are important to her. "The moment *Suits* became successful and I realized people (especially young girls) were listening to what I had to say, I knew I needed to be saying something of value," Meghan said. She has championed gender equality, clean-water campaigns, and pet adoption. In 2015 Meghan spoke at a United Nations (UN) conference on International Women's Day. Later, she became the UN Women's Advocate for Political Participation and Leadership. As part of this role, Meghan traveled to Rwanda. She met with women leaders in the government and discussed issues regarding the country's refugee camps.

In her personal life, Meghan had some difficulties with romance. She married film producer Trevor Engelson in 2011, but the marriage did not last. After just two years, they divorced. Meghan was still looking for the right partner.

A Whirlwind Romance

In June 2016, Meghan's life would change in an unexpected way. That's when she met Harry on a blind date set up by a mutual friend. Despite both Harry and Meghan being in the public eye, they didn't know much about each other before the date. Though she had certainly heard of the prince before they met, Meghan just wanted to know if he was nice. Harry had not seen *Suits* before he met Meghan.

During their date, Meghan and Harry hit it off immediately. It was the beginning of their whirlwind romance. Harry asked Meghan for another date the

Harry and Meghan on a date watching the 2017 Invictus Games in Toronto

following day. During this date, Harry persuaded Meghan to travel to Africa with him. While there, they camped out under the stars. The trip gave them time to get to know each other out of the spotlight.

Just four months after their first date, on October 31, 2016, news got out that Harry and Meghan were in a relationship. The tabloids ran wild as reporters speculated about the romance. Reporters and photographers lurked outside Meghan's mother's house, and they even tried to gain illegal entry to Meghan's home. The media bombarded nearly every one of Meghan's friends, coworkers, or loved ones with interview requests.

The tabloids also wrote about Meghan's biracial identity in a negative way. The mixture of harassment, sexism, and racism in the articles was alarming to the couple. On November 8, Harry released a public statement confirming the relationship and asking the press to stop harassing Meghan and printing negative articles about her. Harry was all too familiar with tabloid culture, but Meghan, despite being an actor, was completely unprepared for the onslaught of media coverage. Harry wanted to protect her from it if he could.

The couple kept their relationship private as much as possible. With Meghan's filming schedule and Harry's charity work, the couple had to maintain a long-distance relationship. They split their time between London and Toronto, where *Suits* was filmed. They frequently traveled to spend time with each other outside of the public eye. Together, they visited Botswana, Norway, and Jamaica.

Harry and Meghan announce their engagement at the garden at Kensington Palace, London.

Harry introduced Meghan to members of his family, including Queen Elizabeth. Meghan said, "It's incredible to be able to meet her through his lens, not just with his honor and respect for her as the monarch, but the love that he has for her as his grandmother. She's an incredible woman."

After dating for a little more than a year, Harry knew he had found the woman he wanted to marry. In early November 2017, the couple was roasting a chicken for dinner and having a quiet night in Nottingham Cottage, their small home on the grounds of Kensington Palace. Harry got down on one knee to propose. Excited and nervous, Meghan tried to say yes before Harry had even finished the proposal. The couple officially announced their engagement on November 27, 2017.

Both families were thrilled about the engagement. Meghan's parents said, "We are incredibly happy for Meghan and Harry. Our daughter has always been a kind and loving person. To see her union with Harry, who shares the same qualities, is a source of great joy for us as parents." Harry's family also sent their congratulations to the couple.

The couple married on May 19, 2018. They were wed at St. George's Chapel at Windsor Castle in England. Since

Harry and Meghan kiss underneath a flower arch during their wedding.

it was a private wedding and not a state event, the couple did not invite political leaders. Instead, the six hundred guests were a diverse mix of royal family, friends, and celebrities.

All eyes were on Meghan as she climbed the steps of Windsor Castle. She wore an elegant white gown and a long, lace-trimmed veil. Her father could not attend the wedding for health reasons, so Meghan walked by herself halfway down the aisle. Then Harry's father joined Meghan and walked with her to the front of the chapel where Harry was waiting in his military uniform. The ceremony was infused with several American elements. The Reverend Michael Curry, the first African American head of the Episcopal Church, delivered an emotional and stirring sermon. Later, two hundred guests attended a dinner reception hosted by Charles, which was capped off by a colorful fireworks display.

Royal Tour

After their wedding, Harry and Meghan received new titles: Duke and Duchess of Sussex. As part of the royal family, they had duties such as attending official events, meeting with foreign diplomats, and speaking at ceremonies. Harry and Meghan's first day on the job had them attending a ceremony celebrating Charles's seventieth birthday. Soon the couple was thrown into a whirlwind of work.

In October the couple arrived in Sydney for their royal tour of Australia and several neighboring countries. When Harry and Meghan's plane landed, people rushed to meet them. Some young fans waited outside Sydney Opera House with signs that declared their love for the royal couple. One young fan even made a pasta necklace, which he gave to Meghan. She wore the gift proudly around her neck while attending a reception at the Melbourne Government House.

Meghan wearing a pasta necklace a young fan made for her

The couple's royal tour in Australia and its neighboring countries was important for several reasons. It gave Harry and Meghan the chance to improve relations between governments. It also gave them a chance to speak on topics personal to them. The Invictus Games, a worldwide athletic competition for wounded military veterans, were being held that year in Sydney. Harry spoke at the opening ceremony. As a veteran himself, Harry's words were impassioned, and they resonated deeply with the service members in the audience.

During their stop in Suva, Fiji, Meghan gave a speech to students and staff at the University of the South Pacific.

She talked about the importance of having open access to education, particularly for girls in developing countries. Meghan admitted that she was only able to attend college with the help of scholarships, financial aid, and work-study programs. College was a valuable experience for her, and she wants to increase access to higher education for all women.

The couple ended their royal tour in New Zealand, but not before having a little fun with the locals. Harry and Meghan participated in a welly-wanging contest with a group of children, where they competed to see who could throw a rubber boot the farthest. The game took place during a ceremony in Redvale, New Zealand, where 49 acres (20 ha) of land would be dedicated to conservation. The duke and duchess played on opposite teams. They both tried to one-up each other by throwing the boot farther, but eventually Meghan's team won.

Meghan tossing a rubber boot in a welly-wanging contest

Harry, Meghan, and Archie visiting South Africa in September 2019

Welcome to the Family

Harry and Meghan's son, Archie Harrison, was born on May 6, 2019, at Portland Hospital in London. The couple was thrilled. Across the ocean, Meghan's mother was overjoyed for her daughter. Queen Elizabeth and Charles were also delighted for the couple and sent their congratulations.

Despite the new addition to the family, life began to slowly worsen for Meghan as part of the royal family. Since marrying Harry, she had been struggling with her mental health. Even after getting married, tabloids continued to target her. They called her ambitious, a trait that she formerly saw as positive, for marrying a prince. "Apparently ambition is a terrible, terrible thing, for a woman–that is according to some," she reflected on her podcast. "So, since I've felt the negativity behind it, it's really hard to un-feel it. I can't unsee it either, in the millions of girls and women who make themselves smaller–so much smaller–on a regular basis."

Meghan did not feel that she could count on her new family to protect her from the press. As a member of the royal family, she had to maintain a clean public image. That meant she couldn't appear angry or talk back to reporters, even when they published falsehoods about her. Harry tried to convince his family to help take the heat off Meghan. However, some royal family members felt it

Meghan had her own podcast called *Archetypes*. The podcast interviewed guests about stereotypes and labels leveled against women. It aired from August 2022 to June 2023.

Harry and Meghan visit Tembisa Township in South Africa to learn more about their youth employment services.

was unfair for his wife to receive special treatment when their own spouses faced similar tabloid scrutiny.

When Archie was four months old, he traveled to South Africa with his parents for a royal function. Harry and Meghan left Archie with his nanny so the couple could attend an official event, and a fire broke out in the nursery. Archie and the nanny were safe, but Harry and Meghan were distraught when they found out their son had nearly been harmed. Despite being shaken, Harry and Meghan didn't allow tabloid photographers to see how upset they were.

In October 2019, a media company in London called Associated Newspapers published parts of a private letter Meghan had written to her father. Angered by the invasion of privacy, Meghan sued Associated Newspapers and accused the company of unlawfully publishing her letter. She and Harry also cut ties with several major United Kingdom tabloids.

Days after the letter was published, Harry and Meghan decided to step back from the public spotlight. They spent six weeks under the radar, quietly vacationing on Vancouver Island in Canada. Harry and Meghan had spent the previous two Christmases in Sandringham, Queen Elizabeth's country home, but in 2019, the couple wanted a quieter holiday. They decided to celebrate Christmas with Meghan's family in the United States. Then, early in the new year, Harry and Meghan returned to public life with shocking news. They were stepping down from the royal family.

Stepping Down

On January 8, 2020, Harry and Meghan announced their decision to step down from their roles as senior members of the royal family. Just days after their announcement, the royal family called an emergency meeting. Harry, Charles, and William met with Queen Elizabeth at Sandringham House in England. After a tense, ninety-minute discussion, the queen announced that the family would be supportive of Harry and Meghan's decision.

In March the couple officially exited their royal life. Despite the big event, their exit was overshadowed by the global spread of the deadly disease COVID-19 and

Harry and Meghan live with their children in Santa Barbara, California (*above*).

the widespread social lockdowns that followed. Right as the pandemic was getting serious, Harry and Meghan took Archie to the United States. They stayed with actor and movie producer Tyler Perry, a family friend, at his mansion in Beverly Hills, California. In July Harry and Meghan moved into their own home in Santa Barbara, California. Life away from the British monarchy was healing for the couple. The pandemic's stay-at-home orders meant they could live quietly, without cameras constantly pointed at them. They spent valuable time with Archie.

In September Harry and Meghan signed a five-year, $100 million contract with Netflix to produce documentaries, scripted shows, and other content. In February 2021, the couple announced they were having a second child. Archie would become a big brother.

Less than a month later, Harry and Meghan dropped a bombshell in an interview with Oprah Winfrey. In the high-profile interview, the couple sat across from Oprah on a beautiful outdoor patio. They revealed that instances of racism, constant tabloid pressure, and the rigid demands of royal life caused them to leave the UK. Meghan's biggest regret from her time with the royal family was learning that they would not protect her.

A London newspaper headlining Harry and Meghan's interview with Oprah

"I came to understand that not only was I not being protected, but that they were willing to lie to protect other members of the family. They weren't willing to tell the truth to protect me and my husband." She said some family members even expressed concerns about "how dark [Archie's] skin might be" when he was born.

The candid interview shocked the public. Very few people knew about the inner workings of Buckingham Palace, the official residence of the British monarch. Fewer were able to talk about it. Harry and Meghan's interview shed some light on the royal family.

On June 4, 2021, Lilibet Diana was born to Harry and Meghan at Santa Barbara Cottage Hospital. She was named after Queen Elizabeth, whose nickname was Lilibet, and Diana, Harry's mother. A new era for the former royal couple had arrived.

Lilibet's Baptism

Unlike Archie, who was baptized at Queen Elizabeth's private chapel at Windsor Castle, Lilibet was baptized in Los Angeles. Roughly thirty guests attended the event, including Meghan's mother, Doria; Lilibet's godfather, Tyler Perry; and an unnamed godmother. Perry flew in from Atlanta, Georgia, bringing a ten-person gospel choir with him. They sang "Oh Happy Day" and "This Little Light of Mine" at Lilibet's special event.

New Era

Even after leaving the royal family, Harry remained close with Queen Elizabeth. In June 2022, he and Meghan attended the Queen's Platinum Jubilee celebrating her seventy-year reign. The couple was no longer actively part of the royal family—though they did keep their duke and duchess titles—so they did not participate in public events with the family. Queen Elizabeth also declined an appearance during the Platinum Jubilee due to poor health. Harry and Meghan privately paid their respects to her.

Harry and Meghan attend Queen Elizabeth's Platinum Jubilee.

Center row, left to right: William, Harry, and Peter Philips (their cousin) walk behind Charles at Queen Elizabeth's funeral.

In September the queen's health failed, and she died at the age of ninety-six at Balmoral Castle in Scotland. Harry and Meghan arrived to say their goodbyes. The royal family later held a funeral procession for the late queen in Westminster Abbey. Thousands of members of the British armed forces took part in the procession. Thousands more people crowded the streets along the 2-mile (3.2 km) walk to pay their respects to the late queen. William and Harry walked with other members of the royal family behind the coffin, the same way they did during their mother's funeral procession.

The queen's death meant big changes in the royal family. Charles, Harry's father, became the new monarch of the British Commonwealth. Camilla became the queen consort. William and Kate took the titles the Prince and Princess of Wales and Duke and Duchess of Cornwall. Harry and Meghan did not get new titles. However, Archie and Lilibet became prince and princess.

In December 2022, a long-awaited documentary series about Harry and Meghan premiered on Netflix. The first three hour-long episodes aired on December 8. The final three were released one week later. The series follows the two from their childhoods to the royal

King Charles and Queen Consort Camilla greeting the public after Charles's coronation

family and beyond. Harry and Meghan were able to tell their story like never before. Shortly after, Harry's memoir, *Spare*, was published on January 10, 2023. In the book, he reveals many personal details, including information on his relationships with the media, his mother, and his wife and facts about his separation from the royal family. On May 6, 2023, Harry attended King Charles's coronation alone. Meghan stayed in California to celebrate Archie's birthday with Lilibet.

Balanced Schedule

Harry and Meghan are a team when it comes to their children. While one parent is making breakfast, the other gets the kids ready for the day. Since the COVID-19 pandemic began, the couple has worked from home, giving them more time to spend with their children. But even as they're focusing on their kids, they don't forget to take care of themselves.

Harry described what he does with his personal time when he isn't working or parenting. "One of the kids has gone to school. The other one's taking a nap. There's a break in our program. It's either [I] work out, take the dog for a walk, get out in nature, maybe meditate." Juggling two kids is a lot for any parent. But Harry and Meghan make the best of work and parenting by having a well-balanced schedule.

The Bench

Harry isn't the only writer in the family. In 2021 Meghan published *The Bench*, a picture book for children. The book is about the touching relationship between a father and son told from the perspective of the mother. It's illustrated by Christian Robinson and features watercolor art. Meghan dedicated the book to Harry and Archie, and it was released just days after Lilibet's birth.

Harry and Meghan's relationship has been through many ups and downs. But they've been a team through all of it. In the years following their first date, they created a home, a family, and eventually a life free from the pressures of being a royal. "I have no doubt that my mom would be incredibly proud of me," Harry said. "I'm living the life that she wanted to live for herself, living the life that she wanted us to be able to live."

Important Dates

1981   Meghan Markle is born on August 4.

1984   Harry is born on September 15.

1996   Charles and Diana are divorced.

1997   Diana dies in a car crash.

2003   Meghan graduates from Northwestern University. Harry graduates from Eton College.

2005   Harry begins his training at the Royal Military Academy Sandhurst.

2007   Harry begins duty in Afghanistan.

2011   Meghan appears as a leading character on the television show *Suits*. She marries film producer Trevor Engelson.

2013   Meghan divorces Trevor Engelson.

2015	Harry ends his official military duties.
2017	Harry and Meghan announce their engagement on November 27.
2018	The royal wedding takes place on May 19 at St. George's Chapel at Windsor Castle.
2019	Archie Harrison is born on May 6.
2020	Harry and Meghan officially exit the royal family in March. They move to California.
2021	Lilibet Diana is born on June 4.
2022	Queen Elizabeth II dies in September. Harry and Meghan release their Netflix special in December.
2023	Harry's memoir, *Spare*, is published on January 10. Charles is crowned king on May 6.

Source Notes

8   Li Cohen, "New Trailer for 'Harry & Meghan' Docuseries Teases the 'Full Truth' behind the Couple's Relationship with the Royal Family," CBS News, updated December 5, 2022, https://www.cbsnews.com/news/harry-and-meghan-netflix-series-new-trailer-royal-family-full-truth/.

12–13   Britt Stephens, "30 Sweet, Heartbreaking Things William and Harry Have Said about Princess Diana," PopSugar, September 27, 2017, https://www.popsugar.com/celebrity/Prince-William-Prince-Harry-Quotes-About-Princess-Diana-43341113.

15   "Prince Harry Reveals He 'Wanted Out' of Royal Family Years before Megxit in 2017 Interview," *New Zealand Herald*, May 30, 2023, https://www.nzherald.co.nz/lifestyle/prince-harry-reveals-he-wanted-out-of-royal-family-years-before-megxit-in-2017-interview/2EEZRFDBTBCGNI3UCALDBUTZ7A/.

17–18   Morgan Evans, "Prince Harry Opens Up about the One Place He Feels Most at Home," *Harper's Bazaar*, January 3, 2017, http://www.harpersbazaar.com/culture/features/news/a19694/prince-harry-town-and-country-interview-africa/.

21   Meghan Markle, "Meghan Markle: I'm More Than an 'Other,'" *Elle* (UK), December 12, 2016, http://www.elleuk.com/life-and-culture/news/a26855/more-than-an-other/.

21–22   Markle.

22   Meghan Markle, "Meghan Markle for *ELLE*: 'With Fame Comes Opportunity, but Also a Responsibility,'" *Elle* (UK), November 8, 2016, http://www.elleuk.com/life-and-culture/elle-voices/articles/a32612/meghan-markle-fame-comes-responsibility.

25   Morgan Evans, "A Definitive History of Prince Harry and Meghan Markle's Royal Relationship," *Town and Country*, December 8, 2022, http://www.townandcountrymag.com/society/a9664508 /prince-harry-meghan-markle-relationship/.

26   Katie Frost, "Prince Harry and Meghan Markle Are Engaged!," *Town and Country*, November 27, 2017, https://www .townandcountrymag.com/society/tradition/a12198435/prince -harry-meghan-markle-engaged/.

31   Skyler Caruso, "Meghan Markle's Biggest Revelations in Her 'Archetypes' Podcast," *People*, updated October 25, 2022, https://people.com/royals/meghan-markle-biggest-revelations -in-archetypes-podcast/.

36   Jessica Sager, "Prince Harry and Meghan Markle's Relationship Timeline," *People*, May 18, 2023, https://people.com/royals /prince-harry-meghan-markle-romance-timeline/.

40   Julie Tremaine, "All about Prince Harry and Meghan Markle's Children," *People*, updated June 14, 2023, https://people.com /parents/prince-harry-and-meghan-markle-children/.

41   Tremaine.

Selected Bibliography

Harry & Meghan. Directed by Liz Garbus. Netflix, 2022. https://www.netflix.com/search?q=harry%20and%20&tjbv=81439256.

Junor, Penny. *Prince Harry: Brother, Soldier, Son*. New York: Grand Central, 2014.

Larcombe, Duncan. *Prince Harry: The Inside Story*. New York: HarperCollins, 2017.

Morton, Andrew. *Diana: Her True Story—in Her Own Words*. New York: Simon & Schuster, 2017.

Nicholl, Katie. *Harry: Life, Loss, and Love*. New York: Hachette, 2018.

———. *William and Harry: Behind the Palace Walls*. New York: Hachette, 2010.

Petit, Stephanie. "A Complete Timeline of Meghan Markle and Prince Harry's Exit from Royal Life." *People*. Updated June 29, 2023. https://people.com/royals/meghan-markle-prince-harry-step-down-royal-life-timeline/.

Simmons, Simone, and Ingrid Seward. *Diana: The Last Word*. New York: St. Martin's, 2005.

Wilson, A. N. *The Queen*. New York: Atlantic Books, 2016.

Yang, Lucy. "40 Candid Photos from Prince Harry and Meghan Markle's Royal Tour." Insider, October 31, 2018. https://www.insider.com/prince-harry-meghan-markle-royal-tour-australia-new-zealand-photos-2018-10.

Learn More

Bolte, Mari. *King Charles III: Claiming the British Crown.* Minneapolis: Lerner Publications, 2023.

Britannica Kids: Meghan Markle
https://kids.britannica.com/kids/article/Meghan-Markle/631675

Britannica Kids: Prince Harry
https://kids.britannica.com/kids/article/Prince-Harry/476271

Kawa, Katie. *Meghan Markle: Making a Difference as a Duchess.* New York: KidHaven, 2021.

Kiddle: British Royal Family Facts for Kids
https://kids.kiddle.co/British_royal_family

Stine, Megan. *Who Is Queen Elizabeth II?* New York: Penguin Workshop, 2021.

Index

Photo Acknowledgments

Image credits: Karwai Tang/Getty Images, p. 2; Kevin Mazur/Getty Images Entertainment/Getty Images, p. 6; Jonathan Brady - PA Images/Getty Images, p. 8; Tim Graham Photo Library/Getty Images, p. 9; Princess Diana Archive/Stringer/Getty Images, p. 11; Mark Cuthbert/UK Press/Getty Images, p. 14; Anwar Hussein Collection/ROTA/WireImage/Getty Images, p. 15; UPI/Kirsty Wigglesworth/Pool/Alamy, p. 16; Ian Vogler - Pool/Getty Images, p. 17; Samir Hussein/WireImage/Getty Images, pp. 19, 37, 38; Michael Stewart/WireImage/Getty Images, p. 21; AP Photo/KGC-22/STAR MAX/IPx, p. 23; AP Photo/Dominic Lipinski/PA Wire, p. 25; Ben STANSALL/POOL/AFP/Getty Images, p. 26; Scott Barbour/Stringer/Getty Images, p. 28; Pool/Samir Hussein/WireImage/Getty Images, pp. 29, 30, 32; Raj Valley/Alamy, p. 31; Alexander Spatari/Getty Images, p. 34; Kathy deWitt/Alamy, p. 35; AP Photo/DPPA/Sipa USA, p. 39; Leon Neal/Getty Images, p. 41.

Cover: Albert Nieboer/Netherlands OUT/Point de Vue OUT/dpa/Alamy.